Regina Noel

The BEDTIME Rhyme

with illustrations by
Mathew Havran

TEACUP PRESS

www.teacup-press.com • www.foxpointepublishing.com/author-regina-noel

Library of Congress Cataloging-in-Publication Data
Noel, Regina, author.
Eckman, Raven, editor.
Havran, Mathew, illustrator.
Town, Scotty, designer.

The Bedtime Rhyme / Regina Noel. – First edition.

Summary: An illustrated lullaby that will help foster loving and healthy family communication.

ISBN 978-1-955743-52-5 (hardcover) / 978-1-955743-37-2 (softcover)
[1. Emotions & Feelings – Fiction. 2. Music – Fiction. 3. Family – Fiction.
4. Social Themes – Fiction. 5. Bedtime & Dreams – Fiction.]

Library of Congress Control Number: 2 0 2 1 9 1 8 4 2 0

Second printing - November 2025

To my Dear Simone and Charles.
I like you just as you are,
always and forever.

To the Mamas, Papas, and Caregivers,

Bedtime is one of the most crucial times of the day for our littles, and sometimes the most challenging. It can raise real fears over separation. And just like adults, children need time to "come down" from the day. They need structure and regular bedtime rituals.

It is best to plan a full half hour of connectedness—after the normal bedtime ritual of teeth brushing, baths, and going to the bathroom. This should center around one-on-one time while they are in their bed, ready for sleep. Books, cuddles, and conversations about the day are vital to helping our littles feel safe and secure in their own space.

Knowing you are there watching out for them—even if you aren't "right" there, will ease any separation anxiety they may have. Being present to their world and knowing the right things to say to build our children up are crucial to a good night's sleep and a successful day ahead.

This book includes what I believe are the most important things a child needs to feel loved, connected, supported, and safe: a cuddle, your listening, your voice, and the most important thing a child wants to know—

"I like you just as you are!"

How very poignant! Isn't that all any of us want? To be liked and accepted for who we are?

It is important to note that when listening to our children share, we must not be judgmental. We may have different ideas of what our littles should or shouldn't be doing or liking. But can you remember having different ideas of what you wanted with your life? Ideas that differed from what your parents or caregivers wanted for you? Do you remember feeling their unhappiness surrounding your likes and dislikes? If we felt it, and remember it, it is almost a guarantee that our children will feel it, too. And if we want them to share hard things with us as they grow, we must practice with the small stuff each day.

The best way to be connected with our littles is to truly grasp the concept of "I like you just as you are." No judgments, no right or wrong. Just pure acceptance of our beautiful, growing charges.

Here's to you, doing the best you can.

And know that I too, like YOU, just as you are!

1

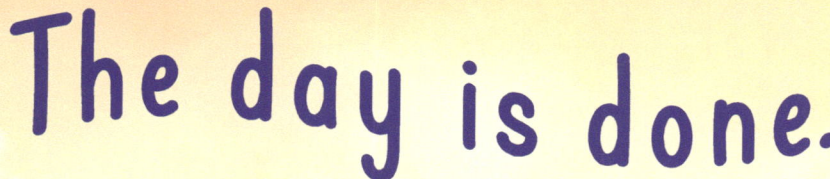

The day is done.

We've had some fun!

Now grab your teddy,
AND LET'S GET READY.

For now it's time for our
BEDTIME RHYME. . .

But before we begin,
I'D LIKE TO KNOW. . .

What made you SAD,

and what made you GLAD?

It's your turn to
SHARE,

Thank you for that.
IT WILL ALWAYS BE TRUE. . . .

I love learning
ALL ABOUT YOU!

Now it's my turn to share.

14

Listen closely and hug your bear. . .

The STARS are out,

the NIGHT has come,

and now we go to sleep.

18

But not without a cuddle or two.

I'll keep you safe,

23

from all you FEAR. . .

I'm always near.

25

I've one last thing

to SHARE
with you. . .

in the midnight blue.

I like you just as you are . . .

and I do.

PLAY ALONG!

(Ukulele chords)

(Ukulele notes)

THE BEDTIME RHYME

Regina Noel

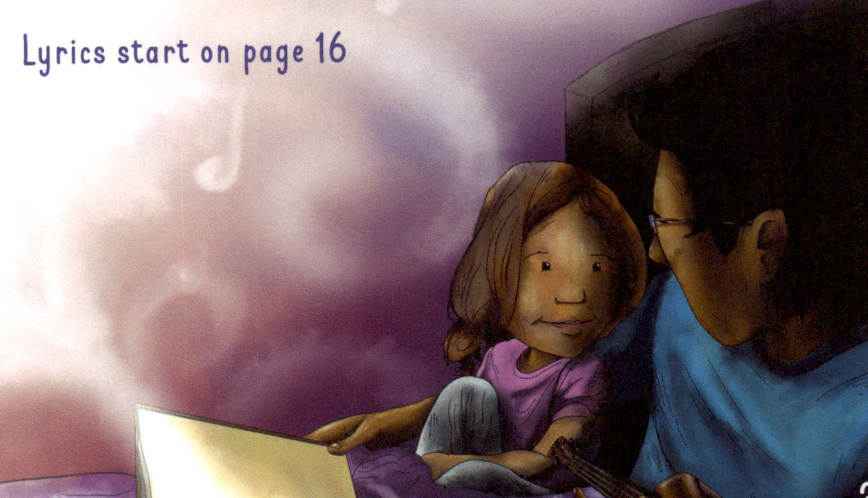

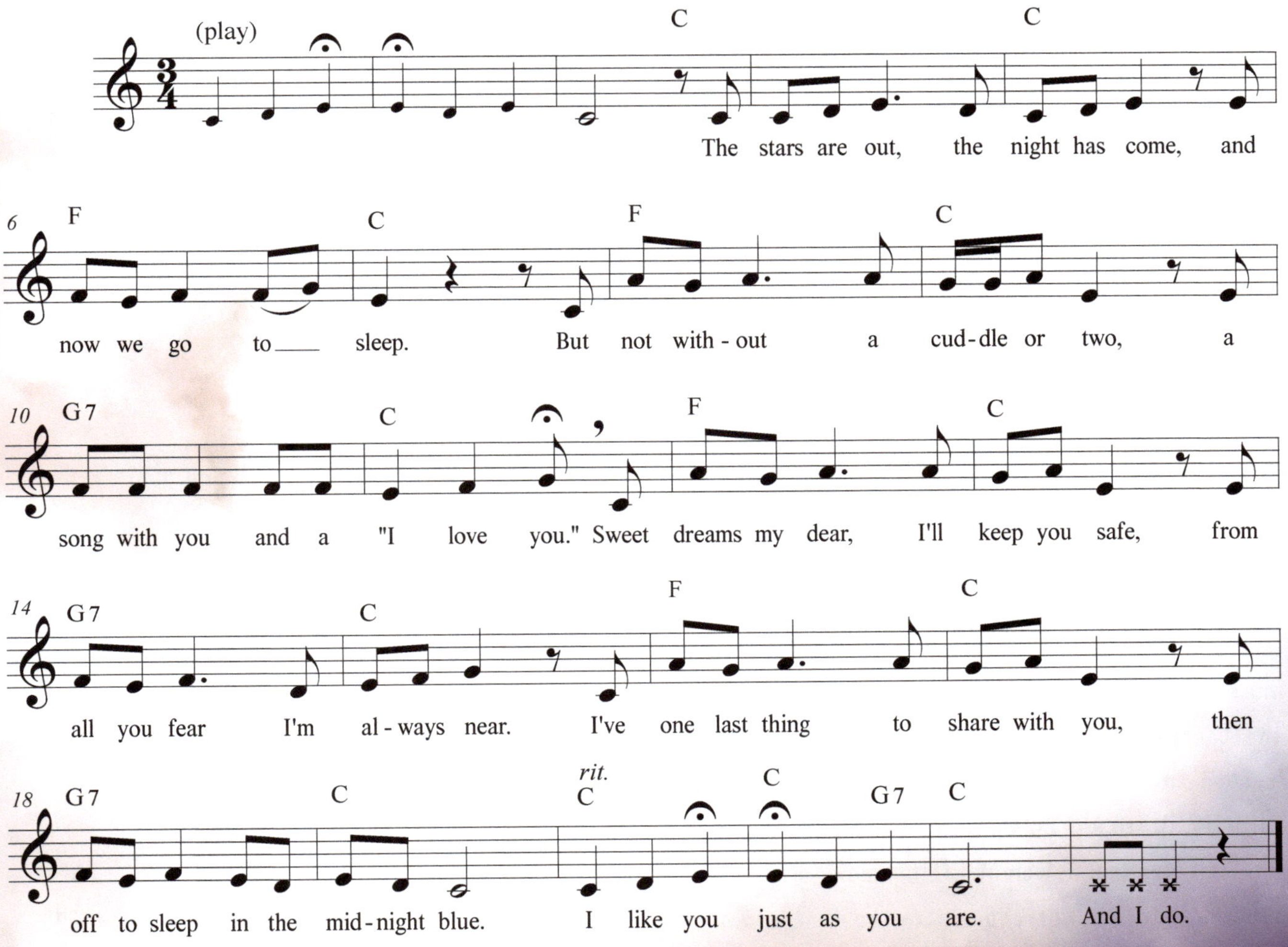
(play)
C C
The stars are out, the night has come, and
6 F C F C
now we go to___ sleep. But not with - out a cud-dle or two, a
10 G7 C F C
song with you and a "I love you." Sweet dreams my dear, I'll keep you safe, from
14 G7 C F C
all you fear I'm al - ways near. I've one last thing to share with you, then
18 G7 C rit. C C G7 C
off to sleep in the mid-night blue. I like you just as you are. And I do.

Lyrics start on page 16

MEET THE CREATORS...

Photo credit: Nate Troy & Sara Stromseth-Troy

ABOUT THE AUTHOR

Regina Noel

Regina Noel resides in Iowa with her two children and two dogs. She holds a BA in Music and Physical Education from Luther College, as well as an MA in Elementary Education from Grand Canyon University. Ms. Regina is the owner and instructor of the Regina Noel Music Studio, where she teaches private piano, voice, and ukulele lessons to children and adults of all ages and abilities. When she isn't teaching or writing, you can find Ms. Regina weight lifting, making music, making (and eating) chocolates, or just plain hanging out with her kiddos and doggos.

ABOUT THE ILLUSTRATOR

Mathew Havran

Mathew Havran of Decorah, Iowa is fairly new to the world of illustrating children's books, but not to drawing and painting. A self-taught artist since kindergarten, drawing quickly became his favorite pastime up into the present. Today, some of his other hobbies include playing the piano and ukulele, rollerblading, singing and beatboxing, and family-fun activities with his wife and two kids. He currently makes a living as a Test Technician at Collins Aerospace but has been devoting much of his free time to illustrating, painting, and muraling in his community. Much of his work can be seen around Decorah and on his Facebook page, "Artist Mathew Havran."